THANK YOU TEACHER

Bath • New York • Cologne • Melbourne • Delhi
Hong Kong • Shenzhen • Singapore • Amsterdam

You won't be my teacher next year!

So this book is a
BIG THANK YOU
to you,

....

for **all** that you've taught me ...

And because you've taught me **A LOT** of things, **I've drawn a picture of you.**

I WANT TO THANK YOU FOR YOUR...

Enthusiasm

LOVE OF READING

KINDNESS

PATIENCE

1.
....
....
....
....

SMILE

2.
....
....
....
....

3.
....
....
....
....

GOOD ADVICE

encouragement

And it wasn't EVEN hard coming up with three things.

I've asked around,
and these seem to
be the **main reasons**
why you have to
go to school ...

1. To make new **friends.**

2.

To get a good start in life.

1 2 3 4 5

3. To find out about the **world**.

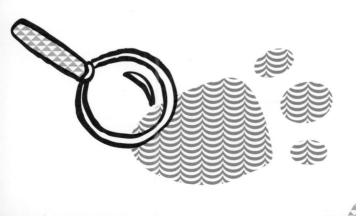

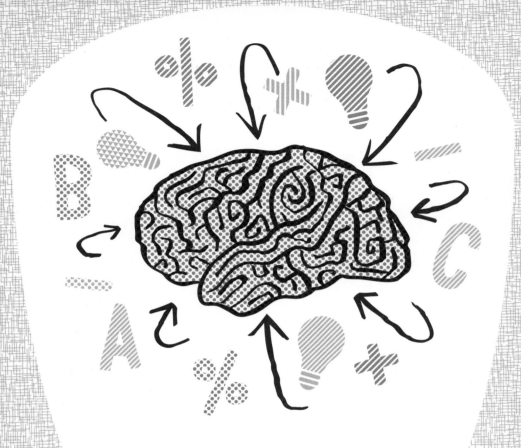

4. To make you **smart.**

5.
It's the LAW!

These are some
of the awesome
things that I've learned
in your class:

So you must be **amazingly** smart.

I'd like to be that smart one day.

Before I met you,
I was **smaller** and had
LOADS to learn.

Having spent time with you,
I know WAY MORE things.

This is me now:
Really Confident!

The thing is, you know

WHAT'S WHAT

and you always have

a GREAT answer ...

... Whether it's about the world we live in

... How to write a good sentence

... Working with numbers

Or:

....

....

....

....

....

You have encouraged

ME to be ME!

I've learned
confidence and self-belief.

I am:

PROUDER

BRAVER

STRONGER

SMARTER

and

. . . .

And it feels
great!

Here are **THREE** reasons
why I'm DIFFERENT now ...

I'm looking forward to carrying on learning loads of **new stuff** ...

... but I'm **kind of sad** it won't be with you.

NEXT YEAR
you'll have your **hands full**
with another class.

But I'm **pretty sure**
they won't be as
nice as my class.

So you'll
be sorry to
SEE US GO!

THANK YOU ⭐

GRACIAS

DANKE

DZIĘKUJĘ

Merci

Grazie

TACK

OBRIGADO

KIITOS

Grazzi

→ **HVALA**

For being a great teacher.

. . . .

signature